Dodie,
From Bob & JANE
WE LoVE You
April 2019

ON
CALVARY'S
HILL

ALSO BY MAX LUCADO

On Calvary's Hill

40 Readings *for the* Easter Season

Max Lucado

Thomas Nelson
Since 1798

Published in Nashville, Tennessee, by Thomas Nelson, an imprint of HarperCollins Christian Publishing, Inc.

Thomas Nelson titles may be purchased in bulk for educational, business, fund-raising, or sales promotional use. For information, please e-mail SpecialMarkets@ ThomasNelson.com.

Unless otherwise noted, Scripture quotations are taken from the New King James Version®. © 1982 by Thomas Nelson. Used by permission. All rights reserved.

Other Scripture references are from the following sources: The Amplified Bible: Old Testament. ©1962, 1964 by Zondervan (used by permission); and Amplified Bible: New Testament. © 1958 by The Lockman Foundation (used by permission) (AMP). Contemporary English Version (CEV). © 1991 by the American Bible Society. Used by permission. *The Message* (MSG) by Eugene H. Peterson. © 1993, 1994, 1995, 1996, 2000. Used by permission of NavPress Publishing Group. All rights reserved. New American Standard Bible® (NASB). © The Lockman Foundation 1960, 1962, 1963, 1968, 1971, 1972, 1973, 1975, 1977, 1995. Used by permission. New Century Version® (NCV). © 2005 by Thomas Nelson. Used by permission. All rights reserved. The Holy Bible, New International Version®, NIV® (NIV). © 1973, 1978, 1984, 2011 by Biblica, Inc.™ Used by permission of Zondervan. All rights reserved worldwide. *Holy Bible*, New Living Translation (NLT). © 1996, 2004, 2007. Used by permission of Tyndale House Publishers, Inc., Wheaton, Illinois 60189. All rights reserved. (Scripture quotations are from the 2007 edition unless otherwise noted.) *The Living Bible* (TLB). © 1971. Used by permission of Tyndale House Publishers, Inc., Wheaton, Illinois 60189. All rights reserved. The New English Bible (NEB) © 1961, 1970, by the Delegates of the Oxford University Press and the Syndics of the Cambridge University Press. Reprinted by permission.

Literary development: Koechel Peterson & Associates, Inc., Minneapolis, Minnesota.

ISBN 978-1-4003-7519-6 (special edition)
ISBN 978-0-8499-6422-0 (e-book)
ISBN 978-0-7180-3132-9 (HC)

Printed in the United States

18 LSC 6 5

Thanks be to God for his indescribable gift!

2 CORINTHIANS 9:15 NIV

CONTENTS

Contents

INTRODUCTION

It's early in the final week. The props and players for Friday's drama are in position. Five-inch spikes are in the bin. A crossbeam leans against a shed wall. The players are nearing the stage—Pilate, Annas and Caiaphas, Judas, the centurions.

Players and props. Only this is no play; it's a divine plan. A plan begun before Adam felt heaven's breath, and now all heaven waits and watches. All eyes are on one figure—the Nazarene.

Commonly clad. Uncommonly focused. Leaving Jericho and walking toward Jerusalem. He doesn't chatter or pause. He's on his final journey.

Even the angels are silent. They know this is no ordinary walk or week. For hinged on this week is the door of eternity.

He knew the end was near. He knew the finality of Friday.

Let's walk with him. Let's see how Jesus spent his final days.

Enter the holy week and observe.

Feel his passion. Sense his power. Hear his promise that death has no power.

Let's follow Jesus on his final journey. For by observing his, we may learn how to make ours.

And the Angels Were Silent

1

THE ROAD TO JERUSALEM

*"Behold, we are going up to Jerusalem, and the Son of Man will be
betrayed to the chief priests and to the scribes; and they will condemn
Him to death, and deliver Him to the Gentiles to mock and to
scourge and to crucify. And the third day He will rise again."*

MATTHEW 20:18–19

The road from Jericho to Jerusalem was just four-
teen miles. A half day's journey. Jesus is at the
front of his band of disciples. A young soldier
marching into battle.

As Jesus states his mission, forget any suggestion that he was trapped and made a miscalculation. Ignore any speculation that the cross was a last-ditch attempt to salvage a dying mission.

These words tell us that Jesus died . . . on purpose. No surprise. No hesitation. No faltering.

The way Jesus marched to his death leaves no doubt: he had come to earth for this moment. The journey to the cross had begun long before leaving Jericho. As the echo of the crunching of the fruit was still sounding in the garden of Eden, Jesus was leaving for Calvary.

Jesus stepped toward Jerusalem with the promise of God in his heart. The divinity of Christ assured the humanity of Christ, and Jesus spoke loud enough for the pits of hell to vibrate: "And the third day He will rise again."

Is there a Jerusalem in your horizon? Are you on a brief journey from painful encounters? Are you only steps away from the walls of your own heartache?

Learn a lesson from your master. The next time you find yourself on a Jericho road marching toward Jerusalem, put the promises of God on your lips. When the blackness of oppression settles around you, draw courage from the Word of God. 'Tis wise to march into Jerusalem with the promise of God in your heart.

And the Angels Were Silent

Lord Jesus, I can't begin to fathom the fact that you purposefully left Jericho, knowing full well that the cross was straight in front of you. Help me to take the Father's promises into my life and to live courageously according to your Word. In Jesus' name, amen.

2

MARY'S EXTRAVAGANT GIFT

Then Mary took a pound of very costly oil of spikenard,
anointed the feet of Jesus, and wiped His feet with her hair.
And the house was filled with the fragrance of the oil.

JOHN 12:3

S he was the only one who believed him. Whenever he spoke of his death, the others shrugged or doubted, but Mary believed. Mary believed because he spoke with a firmness she'd heard before.

"Lazarus, come out!" he'd demanded, and her brother came out. After four days in a stone-sealed grave, he walked out.

And as Mary kissed the now-warm hands of her just-dead brother, she turned and looked. Tear streaks were dry and the teeth shone from beneath the beard. Jesus was smiling.

And in her heart she knew she would never doubt his words.

So when he spoke of his death, she believed.

"Now is the right time," she told herself.

It wasn't an act of impulse. She'd carried the large vial of perfume from her house to Simon's. It wasn't a spontaneous gesture. But it was an extravagant one. The perfume was worth a year's wages. Maybe the only thing of value she had. It wasn't a logical thing to do, but since when has love been led by logic?

Common sense hadn't wept at Lazarus's tomb. Love did, though. Extravagant, risky, chance-taking love.

And now someone needed to show the same to the giver of such love.

So Mary did. She stepped up behind him and stood

with the jar in her hand. She began to pour. Over his head. Over his shoulders. Down his back. She would have poured herself out for him, if she could.

The fragrance of the sweet ointment rushed through the room.

"Wherever you go," the gesture spoke, "breathe the aroma and remember one who cares."

The other disciples mocked her extravagance, but don't miss Jesus' prompt defense of Mary. "Why are you troubling this woman? She did an excellent thing for me."

Jesus' message is just as powerful as it was then: There is a time for risky love. There is a time to pour out your affections on one you love. And when the time comes—seize it, don't miss it.

And the Angels Were Silent

My Lord and Savior, I would love to express my love for you in the extravagant way that Mary did. Help me to pour out my life in worship to you and service to others as a sweet fragrance that brings glory to your most excellent name, Jesus, amen.

3

Jesus Purges the Temple

And He said to them, "It is written, 'My house shall be called a house of prayer,' but you have made it a 'den of thieves.'"

MATTHEW 21:13

It was Passover week. The Passover was the highlight of the Jewish calendar. People came from all regions and many countries to be present for the celebration. Upon arriving, they were obligated to meet two requirements.

First, an animal sacrifice, usually a dove. The dove had to be perfect, without blemish. If you brought a sacrifice from your own source, it would be considered insufficient by the authorities in the temple. So under the guise of keeping the sacrifice pure, the sellers sold doves—at their price.

Second, the people had to pay a yearly temple tax. During Passover, the tax had to be rendered in local currency. Knowing many foreigners would be in Jerusalem to pay the tax, money changers conveniently set up tables and offered to exchange the foreign money for local—for a modest fee, of course.

It's not difficult to see what angered Jesus. Pilgrims journeyed days to see God, to witness the holy, to worship his majesty. But before they were taken into the presence of God, they were taken to the cleaners.

Want to anger God? Get in the way of people who want to see him. Exploit people in the name of God.

In Christ stormed. Doves flapped and tables flew. People scampered and traders scattered.

This was not an impulsive show or temper tantrum. It was a deliberate act with an intentional message. God will never hold guiltless those who exploit the privilege of worship.

Christ's passion on Monday is indignation. There are hucksters in God's house. Remember why Jesus purged the temple. Those closest to it may be the farthest from it.

And the Angels Were Silent

Heavenly Father, work in my life in such a way that people will see you shining forth. Help me to break free from the selfishness and sin that prevent me from being conformed to your image and expressing your holiness. In Jesus' name, amen.

4

JESUS WASHES HIS DISCIPLES' FEET

The evening meal was being served, and the devil had already prompted
Judas Iscariot, son of Simon, to betray Jesus. Jesus . . . got up from the
meal, took off his outer clothing, . . . and began to wash his disciples'
feet, drying them with the towel that was wrapped around him.

JOHN 13:2—5 NIV

It has been a long day. Jerusalem is packed with
Passover guests, most of whom clamor for a glimpse
of the Teacher. The spring sun is warm. The streets

are dry. And the disciples are a long way from home. A splash of cool water would be refreshing.

The disciples enter the room, one by one, and take their places around the table. On the wall hangs a towel, and on the floor sit a pitcher and a basin. Any one of the disciples could volunteer for the job, but not one does.

After a few moments Jesus stands and removes his outer garment. He wraps a servant's girdle around his waist, takes up the basin, and kneels before one of the disciples. He unlaces a sandal and gently lifts the foot, places it in the basin, covers it with water, and begins to bathe it.

One grimy foot after another, Jesus works his way down the row. In Jesus' day the washing of feet was a task reserved not just for servants but for the lowest of servants.

In this case the One with the towel and basin is the King of the universe. Hands that shaped the stars now wash away filth. Fingers that formed mountains now massage toes. And the One before whom all nations will one day kneel now kneels before his disciples. Hours before his own death, Jesus' concern is singular.

He wants his disciples to know how much he loves them.

You can be sure Jesus knows the future of these feet he is washing. These feet will dash for cover at the flash of a Roman sword. Only one pair of feet won't abandon him in the Garden. . . . Judas will abandon Jesus that very night at the table.

What a passionate moment when Jesus silently lifts the feet of his betrayer and washes them in the basin.

Jesus knows what these men are about to do. By morning they will bury their heads in shame and look down at their feet in disgust. And when they do, he wants them to remember how his knees knelt before them and he washed their feet. . . .

He forgave their sin before they even committed it. He offered mercy before they even sought it.

Just Like Jesus

King of the universe, I'd like to think I would have washed your feet and done better than the other disciples, but I know that's not true. Thank you for loving me and washing my feet and offering me mercy when I deserve none. In Jesus' name, amen.

5

IN THE GARDEN

Then they came to a place which was named Gethsemane; and He said to His disciples, "Sit here while I pray." And He took Peter, James, and John with Him, and He began to be troubled and deeply distressed.

MARK 14:32—33

Go with me for a moment to witness what was perhaps the foggiest night in history. The scene is very simple; you'll recognize it quickly. A grove of twisted olive trees. Ground cluttered with large rocks. A low stone fence. A dark, dark night.

Now, look into the picture. Look closely through

the shadowy foliage. See that solitary figure? Flat on the ground. Face stained with dirt and tears. Fists pounding the hard earth. Eyes wide with a stupor of fear. Hair matted with salty sweat. Is that blood on his forehead?

That's Jesus. Jesus in the Garden of Gethsemane.

Maybe you've seen the classic portrait of Christ in the Garden. Kneeling beside a big rock. Snow-white robe. Hands peacefully folded in prayer. A look of serenity on his face. A halo over his head.

The painter didn't use the gospel of Mark as a pattern. When Mark wrote about that painful night, he used phrases such as these: "Horror and dismay came over him," "My heart is ready to break with grief," and "He went forward a little, [and] threw himself on the ground" (14:32–42 NEB).

Mark used black paint to describe this scene. We see an agonizing, straining, and struggling Jesus. We see a "man of sorrows" (Isaiah 53:3 NASB). We see a man struggling with fear, wrestling with commitments, and yearning for relief.

We see Jesus in the fog of a broken heart.

The next time the fog finds you, remember Jesus in the Garden. The next time you think that no one understands or cares, reread the fourteenth chapter of Mark and pay a visit to Gethsemane. And the next time you wonder if God really perceives the pain that prevails on this dusty planet, listen to him pleading among the twisted trees.

The next time you are called to suffer, pay attention.

It may be the closest you'll ever get to God. Watch closely. It could very well be that the hand that extends itself to lead you out of the fog is a pierced one.

No Wonder They Call Him the Savior

Man of sorrows, man of grief, it was for me that you stepped into the horror of bearing my sin. It is incomprehensible that you would take my place and plead for my life. I give you thanks and praise for your ultimate sacrifice. In Jesus' name, amen.

6

Sweat Like Drops of Blood

Jesus . . . kneeled down and prayed, "Father, if you are willing, take away this cup of suffering. But do what you want, not what I want." . . . His sweat was like drops of blood falling to the ground.

Luke 22:41–44 ncv

The writer of Hebrews penned these words: "During the days of Jesus' life on earth, he offered up prayers and petitions with loud cries and tears to the one who could save him from death" (Hebrews 5:7 niv).

It's an expression of Jesus that puzzles us. We've never seen his face like this.

Jesus smiling, yes.

Jesus weeping, absolutely.

Jesus stern, even that.

But Jesus anguished? Cheeks streaked with tears? Face flooded in sweat? Rivulets of blood dripping from his chin?

Jesus was more than anxious; he was afraid. How remarkable that Jesus felt such fear. But how kind that he told us about it. We tend to do the opposite. Gloss over our fears. Cover them up. Keep our sweaty palms in our pockets, our nausea and dry mouths a secret. Not so with Jesus. We see no mask of strength. But we do hear a request for strength.

"Father, if you are willing, take away this cup of suffering." The first One to hear his fear is his Father. He could have gone to his mother or confided in his disciples. He could have assembled a prayer meeting. All would have been appropriate, but none was his priority.

How did Jesus endure the terror of the crucifixion?

He went first to the Father with his tears. He modeled the words of Psalm 56:3: "When I am afraid, I put my trust in you" (NLT 1996).

Do the same with yours. Don't avoid life's Gardens of Gethsemane. Enter them. Just don't enter them alone. And while there, be honest. Pounding the ground is permitted. Tears are allowed. And if you sweat blood, you won't be the first. Do what Jesus did; open your heart.

3:16

Loving Father, I come to you as Jesus did, with all my fears and weaknesses out in the open. I lay down the masks that I hide behind and open my heart to you. Give me the courage to trust in you for all that I face. In Jesus' name, amen.

7

THE BETRAYER

Judas had planned to give them a signal, saying, "The man
I kiss is Jesus. Arrest him." At once Judas went to Jesus
and said, "Greetings, Teacher!" and kissed him.

MATTHEW 26:48–49 NCV

When betrayal comes, what do you do? Get
out? Get angry? Get even? You have to deal
with it some way. Let's see how Jesus dealt
with it.

Begin by noticing how Jesus saw Judas. "Jesus

answered, 'Friend, do what you came to do'" (Matthew 26:50 NCV).

Of all the names I would have chosen for Judas, it would not have been "friend."

What Judas did to Jesus was grossly unfair. There is no indication that Jesus ever mistreated Judas. When, during the Last Supper, Jesus told the disciples that his betrayer sat at the table, they didn't turn to one another and whisper, "It's Judas. Jesus told us he would do this." He had known it, but he treated the betrayer as if he were faithful.

It's even more unfair when you consider that the religious leaders didn't seek him; Judas sought them. "What will you pay me for giving Jesus to you?" he asked (Matthew 26:15 NCV). The betrayal would have been more palatable had Judas been propositioned by the leaders, but he wasn't. He propositioned them.

And Judas's method . . . why did it have to be a kiss?

And why did he have to call him "Teacher"? That's a title of respect.

The incongruity of his words, deeds, and actions— I wouldn't have called Judas "friend." But that is exactly what Jesus called him.

Why? Jesus could see something we can't. He knew Judas had been seduced by a powerful foe. He was aware of the wiles of Satan's whispers. He knew how hard it was for Judas to do what was right.

He didn't justify or minimize what Judas did. Nor did he release Judas from his choice. But he did look eye to eye with his betrayer and try to understand.

As long as you hate your enemy, a jail door is closed and a prisoner is taken. But when you try to understand and release your foe from your hatred, then the prisoner is released, and that prisoner is you.

And the Angels Were Silent

O Lord, if you can forgive Judas for his unthinkable betrayal, I know it's possible for me to extend the same to those who have betrayed and hurt me. Free my heart from the bitterness and hatred that keeps me locked up as a prisoner. Help me to love as you love. In Jesus' name, amen.

8

THE BETRAYAL

Judas came there with a group of soldiers and some guards
from the leading priests and the Pharisees.

JOHN 18:3 NCV

I always had the impression that a handful of soldiers arrested Jesus in the Garden of Gethsemane. I was wrong. At minimum two hundred soldiers were dispatched to deal with a single carpenter and his eleven friends!

Also present were "some guards." This was the temple police. They were assigned to guard the holiest place during the busiest time of the year. They must have been among Israel's finest.

And then there was Judas. One of the inner circle. Not only had Satan recruited the Romans and the Jews, he had infiltrated the cabinet. Hell must have been rejoicing. There was no way Jesus could escape. Satan sealed every exit. His lieutenants anticipated every move, except one.

Jesus had no desire to run. He had no intent of escape. He hadn't come to the Garden to retreat. What they found among the trees was no coward; what they found was a conqueror.

When Jesus states to the mob that came to arrest him, "I am he," he reveals his power. His voice flicks the first domino, and down they tumble. These are the best soldiers with Satan's finest plan; yet one word from Jesus, and two hundred fighting men collapse under a noisy pile of shields, swords, and lamps. Don't miss the symbolism here: when Jesus speaks, Satan falls.

It doesn't matter whom the evil one recruits, including one of the original, handpicked apostles.

The best of Satan melts as wax before the presence of Christ.

Has Satan invaded a garden in your life? Has he profaned a holy part of your world? Your marriage? Your purity? Your honesty? If so, let Jesus claim it back. Today. Now. Before you turn the page.

Open the gate to God. He will enter and do what he did at Gethsemane. He will pray, and he will protect.

A Gentle Thunder

O Conquering One, I gladly open wide the gates of my life and ask you to enter. You see where the Enemy has invaded and done his damage. Come, Lord Jesus, come, and speak your words of truth and power into my life and cleanse my temple. In your name, Jesus, amen.

9

PETER DENIES
KNOWING JESUS

"Everyone else may stumble . . . but I will not."

MATTHEW 26:33 NCV

P eter had bragged, yet he fell. He did what he swore he wouldn't do. He had tumbled face-first into the pit of his own fears. A war raged within the fisherman.

At that moment the instinct to survive collided

with his allegiance to Christ, and for just a moment allegiance won. Peter stood and stepped out of hiding and followed the noise till he saw the torch-lit jury in the courtyard of Caiaphas.

He stopped near a fire and warmed his hands. Other people near the fire recognized him. "You were with him," they challenged. "You were with the Nazarene." Three times people said it, and each time Peter denied it. And each time Jesus heard it.

Please understand that the main character in this drama of denial is not Peter but Jesus. Jesus, who knows the hearts of all people, knew the denial of his friend. Three times the salt of Peter's betrayal stung the wounds of the Messiah.

How do I know Jesus knew? Because of what he did. Then "the Lord turned and looked straight at Peter" (Luke 22:61 NIV). When the rooster crowed, Jesus turned. His eyes searched for Peter and they found him. At that moment there were no soldiers, no accusers, no priests. At that predawn moment in Jerusalem there were only two people—Jesus and Peter.

Peter would never forget that look. Though the look had lasted only a moment, it lasted forever.

He Still Moves Stones

Gracious Father, give me an understanding of what it means to truly have a relationship with your Son. Help me to stay so close to Jesus that I can see his face, even when I fail. Tune my heart into what brings him joy as well as pain. In Jesus' name, amen.

10

ON TRIAL
BEFORE PILATE

Now Jesus stood before the governor. And the governor
asked Him, saying, "Are You the King of the Jews?"
Jesus said to him, "It is as you say."

MATTHEW 27:11

The most famous trial in history is about to begin.
Two soldiers lead the judge down the stone
stairs of the fortress into the broad courtyard.
A regal chair is placed on a landing five steps up from

the floor. The magistrate ascends and takes his seat. The accused is brought into the room and placed below him. A covey of robed religious leaders follows, walks over to one side of the room, and stands.

Pilate looks at the lone figure. "Are you the King of the Jews?"

For the first time, Jesus lifts his eyes. He doesn't raise his head, but he lifts his eyes. He peers at the procurator from beneath his brow. Pilate is surprised at the tone in Jesus' voice.

"Those are your words."

Before Pilate can respond, the knot of Jewish leaders mocks the accused.

Pilate doesn't hear them. *Those are your words.* No defense. No explanation. No panic.

How many times has Pilate sat here? It's a curule seat: cobalt blue with thick, ornate legs. The traditional seat of decision. From here he renders decisions.

How many pleas has he received? How many wide eyes have stared at him, pleading for mercy, begging for acquittal?

But the eyes of this Nazarene are calm, silent.

They don't dart. Pilate searches them for anxiety . . . for anger. He doesn't find it. What he finds makes him shift again.

He's not angry with me. He's not afraid . . . he seems to understand.

Pilate is correct in his observation. Jesus is not afraid, angry, or on the verge of panic, because he is not surprised. Jesus knows his hour and the hour has come.

Pilate is also correct in his question. "What should I do with Jesus, the one called the Christ?" (Matthew 27:22 NCV).

Perhaps you, like Pilate, are curious about this One called Jesus. You are puzzled by his claims and stirred by his passions.

Pilate's question is yours. "What will I do with this man Jesus?"

You have two choices.

You can reject him. You can decide that the idea of God becoming a carpenter is too bizarre—and walk away.

Or you can accept him. You can journey with him. You can listen for his voice and follow him.

And the Angels Were Silent

My Lord and Savior, thank you for inviting me into the journey with you! It is my joy to follow you and to listen for your voice. You are the great and mighty King, and I choose you. In your precious name, Jesus, amen.

11

WASHING OF HANDS

Then he said to them the third time, "Why, what evil has He done? I have found
no reason for death in Him. I will therefore chastise Him and let Him go."
But they were insistent, demanding with loud voices that He be
crucified. And the voices of these men and of the chief priests prevailed.

LUKE 23:22—23

P ilate almost performed what would have been history's greatest act of mercy. He almost pardoned
the Prince of Peace. *Almost.* He had the power. He
had the choice. He wore the signet ring.

But others' voices prevailed. And, as a result, Pilate's

pride prevailed. Pilate's fear prevailed. Pilate's power-hunger prevailed.

Pilate could have heard the voice of Jesus. He could have heard the voice of his wife, who sent him a warning. He could have heard his own voice. He saw through the facade of the trial.

He could have heard other voices. But he didn't. He almost did. But he didn't. Satan's voice prevailed.

His voice often does prevail. Have you heard his wooings?

"One time won't hurt." "She'll never know." "Other people do much worse things."

His rhetoric of rationalization never ends. The father of lies croons and woos.

God, meanwhile, never enters a shouting match with Satan. Truth need not scream. He stands permanently quietly pleading, ever present. No tricks, no temptations, just open proof.

Pilate learned the hard way that this stance of "almost" is suicidal. The other voices will win. Their call is too compelling. And Pilate learned that there is no darker hell than the one of remorse. Washing your hands a thousand times won't free you from the guilt of an opportunity ignored.

Jesus never had room for "almost," and he still doesn't. You are either with him or against him.

No Wonder They Call Him the Savior

Prince of Peace, the voice of the Enemy has been strong over my life, and I've been deceived into believing all sorts of lies. Speak to me now, Lord, and make your voice crystal clear. May it never be said of my life that I *almost* listened and *almost* followed you. I will follow! In Jesus' name, amen.

12

ATONEMENT
FOR SINS

He had to be made like them, fully human in every way, in order
that he might become a merciful and faithful high priest in service to
God, and that he might make atonement for the sins of the people.

HEBREWS 2:17 NIV

Christ lived the life we could not live and took
the punishment we could not take to offer the
hope we cannot resist.

Why?

Jesus was angry enough to purge the temple,

hungry enough to eat raw grain,

distraught enough to weep in public,

fun-loving enough to be called a drunkard,

winsome enough to attract kids,

weary enough to sleep in a storm-bounced boat,

poor enough to sleep on dirt,

radical enough to get kicked out of town,

responsible enough to care for his mother,

tempted enough to know the smell of Satan,

and fearful enough to sweat blood.

Why? Why would heaven's finest Son endure earth's toughest pain? So you would know that "He is able . . . to run to the cry of . . . those who are being tempted and tested and tried" (Hebrews 2:18 AMP).

Whatever you are facing, he knows how you feel.

When you turn to him for help, he runs to you to help. Why? He knows how you feel. He's been there.

He's not ashamed of you. Nor is he confused by you. Your actions don't bewilder him. Your tilted halo doesn't trouble him. So go to him.

Next Door Savior

Son of God, there's nothing I have faced or ever will face that you have not faced, endured, and conquered. And wonder of wonders, you run to me when I need your help. I come to you now. Draw close to me, Jesus. In your name, amen.

13

THE SOLDIERS
WANTED JESUS'
BLOOD

Jesus was beaten with whips and handed over to the soldiers to be crucified.
The governor's soldiers took Jesus into the governor's palace, and
they all gathered around him. . . . Then the soldiers bowed before Jesus
and made fun of him, saying, "Hail, King of the Jews!" They spat
on Jesus. Then they took his stick and began to beat him on the head.
After they finished, the soldiers took off the robe and put his own
clothes on him again. Then they led him away to be crucified.

MATTHEW 27:26–31 NCV

The soldiers? They wanted blood.

So they scourged Jesus. The legionnaire's whip consisted of leather straps with lead balls on each end. His goal was singular: beat the accused within an inch of his death and then stop. Thirty-nine lashes were allowed but seldom needed. A centurion monitored the prisoner's status. No doubt Jesus was near death when his hands were untied and he slumped to the ground.

The whipping was the first deed of the soldiers. The crucifixion was the third. We don't fault the soldiers for these two actions. After all, they were just following orders. But what's hard to understand is what they did in between.

The soldiers' assignment was simple: take the Nazarene to the hill and kill him.

But they had another idea. They wanted to have some fun first. Strong, rested, armed soldiers encircled an exhausted, nearly dead Galilean carpenter and beat up on him. The scourging was commanded. The crucifixion was ordered. But who would draw pleasure out of spitting on a half-dead man?

Spitting isn't intended to hurt the body—it can't. Spitting is intended to degrade the soul, and it does. What were the soldiers doing? Were they not elevating themselves at the expense of another? They felt big by making Christ look small.

Allow the spit of the soldiers to symbolize the filth in our hearts. And then observe what Jesus does with our filth. He carries it to the cross.

Through the prophet he said, "I did not hide my face from mocking and spitting" (Isaiah 50:6 NIV). Mingled with his blood and sweat was the essence of our sin.

God could have deemed otherwise. In God's plan, Jesus was offered wine for his throat, so why not a towel for his face? Simon carried the cross of Jesus, but he didn't mop the cheek of Jesus. Angels were a prayer away. Couldn't they have taken the spittle away?

They could have, but Jesus never commanded them to. For some reason, the One who chose the nails also chose the saliva. Along with the spear and the sponge of man, he bore the spit of man.

The sinless One took on the face of a sinner so that we sinners could take on the face of a saint.

He Chose the Nails

O Lord, Sinless One, is there no low to the level of wretchedness of our hearts? How is it that we draw pleasure from mocking and degrading others? Thank you for carrying the essence of my sin to the cross and nailing it there . . . forever. In Jesus' name, amen.

14

THE CROWN OF THORNS

They took off his clothes and put a red robe on him. Using thorny branches,
they made a crown, put it on his head, and put a stick in his right hand.

MATTHEW 27:28—29 NCV

An unnamed soldier took branches—mature enough to bear thorns, nimble enough to bend—and wove them into a crown of mockery, a crown of thorns.

Throughout Scripture thorns symbolize not sin

but the consequence of sin. Remember Eden? After Adam and Eve sinned, God cursed the land: "So I will put a curse on the ground. . . . The ground will produce thorns and weeds for you, and you will eat the plants of the field" (Genesis 3:17–18 NCV). Brambles on the earth are the product of sin in the heart.

The fruit of sin is thorns—spiny, prickly, cutting thorns.

I emphasize the "point" of the thorns to suggest a point you may have never considered: If the fruit of sin is thorns, isn't the thorny crown on Christ's brow a picture of the fruit of our sin that pierced his heart?

What is the fruit of sin? Step into the briar patch of humanity and feel a few thistles.

Shame. Fear. Disgrace. Discouragement. Anxiety. Haven't our hearts been caught in these brambles?

The heart of Jesus, however, had not. He had never been cut by the thorns of sin.

What you and I face daily, he never knew. Anxiety? He never worried! Guilt? He was never guilty! Fear? He never left the presence of God! Jesus never knew the fruits of sin . . . until he became sin for us.

He did it for you. Just for you.

He Chose the Nails

O Lord, I am well aware of the thorns of sin that pierced you to the heart. Free me from the briars and brambles that keep me locked away from the joy of your presence. In Jesus' name, amen.

15

SIMON FROM CYRENE CARRIES JESUS' CROSS

A man named Simon from Cyrene, the father of Alexander and Rufus, was coming from the fields to the city. The soldiers forced Simon to carry the cross for Jesus.

MARK 15:21 NCV

Four soldiers. One criminal. Four spears. One cross. Simon, a farmer, stands among the crowd and can't see the man's face, only a head wreathed with thorny branches.

The inside corner of the cross saddles the convict's shoulders. Its base drags in the dirt. Its top teeters in the air. The condemned man steadies the cross the best he can but stumbles beneath its weight. He pushes himself to his feet and lurches forward before falling again.

A sour-faced centurion grows more agitated with each diminishing step. He curses the criminal and the crowd. "Hurry up!"

"Little hope of that," Simon says to himself.

The cross-bearer stops in front of Simon and heaves for air. Simon winces at what he sees. The beam rubbing against an already-raw back. Rivulets of crimson streaking the man's face. His mouth hangs open, both out of pain and out of breath.

"His name is Jesus," someone speaks softly.

"Move on!" commands the executioner.

But Jesus can't. His body leans and feet try, but he can't move. The beam begins to sway. Jesus tries to steady it but can't. Like a just-cut tree, the cross begins to topple toward the crowd. Everyone steps back, except the farmer.

Simon instinctively extends his strong hands and catches the cross.

Jesus falls face-first in the dirt and stays there. Simon pushes the cross back on its side. The centurion looks at the exhausted Christ and the bulky bystander and needs only an instant to make the decision. He presses the flat of his spear on Simon's shoulder.

"You! Take the cross!"

Simon dares to object. "Sir, I don't even know the man!"

"I don't care. Take up the cross!"

Simon growls, steps out of the crowd onto the street, and balances the timber against his shoulder, out of anonymity into history, and becomes the first in a line of millions who will take up the cross and follow Christ.

He did literally what God calls us to do figuratively: take up the cross and follow Jesus. "If any of you want to be my followers, you must forget about yourself. You must take up your cross each day and follow me" (Luke 9:23 CEV).

Great Day Every Day

Dear Lord, it was for the joy that was set before you that you endured the cross. I choose this day to take up the cross that you give me and to follow you wherever you lead. I choose to find my joy in you. In Jesus' name, amen.

16

CALVARY

Looking unto Jesus, the author and finisher of our faith, who for
the joy that was set before Him endured the cross, despising the
shame, and has sat down at the right hand of the throne of God.

HEBREWS 12:2

Come with me to the hill of Calvary. Watch as the soldiers shove the carpenter to the ground and stretch his arms against the beams. One presses a knee against a forearm and a spike against a hand. Jesus turns his face toward the nail just as the soldier lifts the hammer to strike it.

Couldn't Jesus have stopped him? With a flex of the biceps, with a clench of the fist, he could have resisted. Is this not the same hand that stilled the sea? Summoned the dead?

But the fist doesn't clench . . . and the moment isn't aborted.

The mallet rings and the skin rips and the blood begins to drip, then rush. Then the questions follow. Why? Why didn't Jesus resist?

"Because he loved us," we reply. That is true, wonderfully true, but—forgive me—only partially true. There is more to his reason. He saw something that made him stay. As the soldier pressed his arm, Jesus rolled his head to the side, and with his cheek resting on the wood, he saw:

A mallet? Yes.

A nail? Yes.

The soldier's hand? Yes.

But he saw something else. Between his hand and the wood, there was a list. A long list of our mistakes: our lusts and lies and greedy moments and prodigal years. A list of our sins.

The bad decisions last year. The bad attitudes from

last week. There, in broad daylight for all of heaven to see, was a list of your mistakes.

He saw the list! He knew the price of those sins was death. He knew the source of those sins was you, and since he couldn't bear the thought of eternity without you, he chose the nails.

3:16

Heavenly Father, you saw the list with my name on it, nailed to the cross with Jesus. Thank you that that long, despicable list was canceled out by Jesus' death and resurrection. It's good to be free! In Jesus' name, amen.

17

THE SIGN ON CHRIST'S CROSS

Now Pilate wrote a title and put it on the cross. And the writing was:

JESUS OF NAZARETH,

THE KING OF THE JEWS.

JOHN 19:19

A hand-painted, Roman-commissioned sign.

Why is a sign placed over the head of Jesus? Why does its wording trouble the Jews, and why does Pilate refuse to change it? Why are the words written in three languages?

Could it be that this piece of wood is a picture of

God's devotion? A symbol of his passion to tell the world about his Son? A reminder that God will do whatever it takes to share with you the message of the sign?

Pilate had intended the sign to threaten and mock the Jews. But God had another purpose . . . Pilate was God's instrument for spreading the gospel. Unknown to himself, he was the amanuensis of heaven. He took dictation from God and wrote it on a sign.

Every passerby could read the sign, for every passerby could read Hebrew, Latin, or Greek—the three great languages of the ancient world. "Hebrew was the language of Israel, the language of religion; Latin the language of the Romans, the language of law and government; and Greek the language of Greece, the language of culture. Christ was declared king in them all."* God had a message for each: "Christ is king." The message was the same, but the languages were different. Since Jesus was a king for all people, the message would be in the tongues of all people.

There is no language he will not speak. Which leads

---

* Isabel McHugh and Florence McHugh, trans., *The Trial of Jesus: The Jewish and Roman Proceedings Against Jesus Christ Described and Assessed from the Oldest Accounts*, by Josef Blinzler (Westminster, MD: The Newman Press, 1959), 1038.

us to a delightful question. What language is he speaking to you? I'm not referring to an idiom or a dialect but to the day-to-day drama of your life. God does speak, you know. He speaks in any language that we will understand.

He Chose the Nails

Great God of the universe, King of the Jews, thank you that you are speaking to me in ways only I can understand. Help me learn to hear your voice in your Word and in all the other ways you speak. In Jesus' name, amen.

18

HE WORE OUR SIN

They divided his clothes among the four of them. They also took his
robe, but it was seamless, woven in one piece from top to bottom.

JOHN 19:23 NLT

It must have been Jesus' finest possession. Jewish
tradition called for a mother to make such a robe
and present it to her son as a departure gift when
he left home. Had Mary done this for Jesus? We don't
know. But we do know the tunic was without seam,
woven from top to bottom. Why is this significant?

Scripture often describes our behavior as the clothes

we wear. Peter urges us to be "clothed with humility" (1 Peter 5:5). David speaks of evil people who clothe themselves "with cursing" (Psalm 109:18). Garments can symbolize character, and like his garment, Jesus' character was uninterrupted perfection.

The character of Jesus was a seamless fabric woven from heaven to earth . . . from God's thoughts to Jesus' compassion. From God's word to Jesus' response. All one piece.

But when Christ was nailed to the cross, he took off his robe of seamless perfection and assumed a different wardrobe, the wardrobe of indignity.

The indignity of nakedness. Stripped before his own mother and loved ones. Shamed before his family.

The indignity of failure. For a few pain-filled hours, the religious leaders were victors, and Christ appeared the loser. Shame before his accusers.

Worst of all, he wore *the indignity of sin.* He "Himself bore our sins in His own body on the tree" (1 Peter 2:24).

The cloth of Christ on the cross? Sin—yours and mine. The sins of all humanity.

3:16

Lord Jesus, I humble myself in your presence and really don't know how to express the wonder I feel. That you would humble yourself to such indignities and shame and wear my sins is love beyond my understanding. Please accept my praise. In your name, amen.

19

CLOSE TO THE CROSS BUT FAR FROM CHRIST

So they said, "Rather than tearing [Jesus' robe] apart, let's throw dice for it."

JOHN 19:24 NLT

There was some dice-throwing that went on at the foot of the cross.

Imagine the scene. The soldiers are huddled in a circle, their eyes turned downward. The criminal above them is forgotten. Casting lots for the possessions of Christ.

Here are common soldiers witnessing the world's most uncommon event, and they don't even know it. As far as they're concerned, he is just another criminal. The cross is forgotten.

It makes me think of us. The religious. Those who claim heritage at the cross. I'm thinking of all of us. Every believer in the land. The stuffy. The loose. The strict. The simple. Upper church. Lower church. "Spirit-filled." Evangelical. Mystical. Literal. Cynical. Robes. Collars. Three-piece suits. Born-againers. Ameners.

I'm thinking we aren't so unlike these soldiers. (I'm sorry to say.)

We, too, play games at the foot of the cross. We compete for members. We scramble for status. We deal out our judgments and condemnations. Competition. Selfishness. Personal gain. It's all there.

So close to the cross, yet so far from the blood.

We are so close to the world's most uncommon

event, but we act like common crapshooters huddled in bickering groups and fighting over silly opinions.

We major in the trivial, constantly finding fault with others. We split into little huddles and then, God forbid, we split again. Another name. Another doctrine. Another "error." Another denomination. Another poker game.

So close to the cross but so far from the Christ.

"May they all be one," Jesus prayed.

One. Not one in groups of two thousand. But one in One. One church. One faith. One Lord. Not Baptist, not Methodist, not Adventist. Just Christians. No denominations. No hierarchies. No traditions. Just Christ.

Once upon a tree, a Creator gave his life for his creation. Maybe all we need are a few hearts who are willing to follow suit.

No Wonder They Call Him the Savior

Gracious Father, I really need to experience your grace at the foot of the cross. Free me from the trappings of religion and help me to discover what it means to be one with Jesus and one with other believers. Just Christ is all I need. In Jesus' name, amen.

20

TWO THIEVES,
TWO CROSSES

And when they had come to the place called Calvary,
there they crucified Him, and the criminals, one
on the right hand and the other on the left.

LUKE 23:33

S kull's Hill—windswept and stony. Two thieves—
gaunt and pale. Jesus is crucified between them.

It's an inexplicable dilemma—how two
people can hear the same words and see the same

Savior, and one see hope and the other see nothing but himself.

With the cynicism of most of the crowd, the one crook called out, "So you're the Messiah, are you? Prove it by saving yourself—and us, too, while you're at it!" (Luke 23:39 TLB).

Perhaps the crook who hurled the barb expected the other crook to take the cue and hurl a few of his own. But he didn't. What the bitter-tongued criminal did hear were words of defense.

"Don't you fear God?"

When it seems that everyone has turned away, a crook places himself between Jesus and the accusers and speaks on his behalf.

"Don't you even fear God when you are dying? We deserve to die for our evil deeds, but this man hasn't done one thing wrong" (Luke 23:40 TLB).

The soldiers look up. The priests cease chattering. Mary wipes her tears and raises her eyes.

Perhaps even Jesus looks at him. Perhaps he turns to see the one who had spoken when all others had remained silent. Perhaps he fights to focus his eyes on the one who offered this final gesture of love he'd receive while alive. I wonder, *Did he smile as this sheep straggled into the fold?*

For that, in effect, is exactly what the criminal is doing. He is stumbling to safety just as the gate is closing. Lodged in the thief's statement are the two facts that anyone needs to recognize in order to come to Jesus.

"We are getting what our deeds deserve. But this man has done nothing wrong" (Luke 23:41 NIV).

Jesus is not on that cross for his sins. He is there for ours.

And once the crook understands this, his request seems only natural. As he looks into the eyes of his last hope, he makes the same request any Christian makes.

"Remember me when you come into your kingdom" (Luke 23:42 NIV).

Six Hours One Friday

Father, thank you for the revelation that came through the one criminal on the cross. I look to Jesus as my only hope of salvation and eternal life, knowing full well that I deserve neither. Thank you for giving me a place in your kingdom. In Jesus' name, amen.

21

THE TALE OF THE
CRUCIFIED CROOK

And Jesus said to him, "Assuredly, I say to you,
today you will be with Me in Paradise."

LUKE 23:43

I f anyone was ever worthless, this one was. If any
man ever deserved dying, this man probably did. If
any fellow was ever a loser, this fellow was at the top
of the list.

Perhaps that is why Jesus chose him to show us
what he thinks of the human race.

Maybe this criminal had heard the Messiah speak. Maybe he had seen him love the lowly. Maybe he had watched him dine with the punks, pickpockets, and potmouths on the streets. Or maybe not. Maybe the only thing he knew about this Messiah was what he now saw: a beaten, slashed, nail-suspended preacher. His face crimson with blood, his bones peeking through torn flesh, his lungs gasping for air.

Something, though, told him he had never been in better company. And somehow he realized that even though all he had was prayer, he had finally met the One to whom he should pray.

"Any chance you can put in a good word for me?" (Loose translation.)

"Consider it done."

Now why did Jesus do that? Why promise this desperado a place of honor at the banquet table? What could this chiseling quisling ever offer in return?

That's the point. Jesus' love does not depend on what we do for him. Not at all. In the eyes of the King, you have value simply because you are. You don't have to look nice or perform well. Your value is inborn.

It makes me smile because I know I don't deserve love like that. None of us do. All of us—even the purest of all—deserve heaven about as much as that crook did. All of us are signing on Jesus' credit card, not ours.

No Wonder They Call Him the Savior

Father, I love that Jesus said "assuredly." The crook needed to know this desperately, and so do I. Thank you for loving me just as I am. I'm looking forward to being with you on "my day." In Jesus' name, amen.

22

"FATHER, FORGIVE THEM"

"Let this Messiah, this king of Israel, come down now from the cross, that we may see and believe." Those crucified with him also heaped insults on him.

MARK 15:32 NIV

O f all the scenes around the cross, this one angers me the most. What kind of people would mock a dying man? Who would be so base as to pour the salt of scorn upon open wounds?

The words thrown that day were meant to wound.

And there is nothing more painful than words meant to hurt.

If you have suffered or are suffering because of someone else's words, you'll be glad to know that there is a balm for this laceration. Meditate on these words: "When they hurled their insults at him, he did not retaliate; when he suffered, he made no threats. Instead, he entrusted himself to him who judges justly" (1 Peter 2:23 NIV).

Jesus did not retaliate or bite back. He did not say, "I'll get you!" "Come on up here and say that to my face!" "Just wait until after the resurrection, buddy!" No, these statements were not found on Christ's lips.

He simply left the judging to God. He did not take on the task of seeking revenge. He demanded no apology. He hired no bounty hunters and sent out no posse. He, to the astounding contrary, spoke on their defense. "Father, forgive them, for they do not know what they are doing" (Luke 23:34 NIV).

And when you think about it, they hadn't the faintest idea what they were doing. They were a stir-crazy mob, mad at something they couldn't see, so they took it out on, of all people, God. But they didn't know what they were doing.

Yes, the dialogue that Friday morning was bitter. The verbal stones were meant to sting. How Jesus, with a body racked with pain, eyes blinded by his own blood, and lungs yearning for air, could speak on behalf of some heartless thugs is beyond my comprehension. Never, never have I seen such love. If ever a person deserved a shot at revenge, Jesus did. But he didn't take it. Instead he died for them. How could he do it? I don't know. But I do know that all of a sudden my wounds seem very painless. My grudges and hard feelings are suddenly childish.

Sometimes I wonder if we don't see Christ's love as much in the people he tolerated as in the pain he endured.

Amazing grace.

No Wonder They Call Him the Savior

Man of sorrows, what a name, for the Son of God who came! Thank you for being despised and forsaken of men that I might know your amazing grace. Hallelujah, what a Savior! In Jesus' name, amen.

23

THE CROSS

God put the wrong on him who never did anything

wrong, so we could be put right with God.

2 CORINTHIANS 5:21 MSG

The cross. Can you turn any direction without seeing one? Perched atop a chapel. Carved into a graveyard headstone. Engraved in a ring or suspended on a chain. The cross is the universal symbol of Christianity. An odd choice, don't you think?

Strange that a tool of torture would come to

embody a movement of hope. The symbols of other faiths are more upbeat: the six-pointed star of David, the crescent moon of Islam, a lotus blossom for Buddhism. Yet a cross for Christianity? An instrument of execution?

Why is the cross the symbol of our faith? To find the answer, look no further than the cross itself. Its design couldn't be simpler. One beam horizontal—the other vertical. One reaches out—like God's love. The other reaches up—as does God's holiness. One represents the width of his love; the other reflects the height of his holiness. The cross is the intersection. The cross is where God forgave his children without lowering his standards.

How could he do this? In a sentence: God put our sin on his Son and punished it there.

Envision the moment. God on his throne. You on the earth. And between you and God, suspended between you and heaven, is Christ on his cross. Your sins have been placed on Jesus. God, who punishes sin, releases his rightful wrath on your mistakes. Jesus receives the blow. Since Christ is between you and God, you don't. The sin is punished, but you are safe—safe in the shadow of the cross.

That describes the width of Christ's love for you. He stretched one hand to the right and the other to the left and had them nailed in that position so you would know he died loving you.

He Chose the Nails

Great God of heaven, thank you for finding a way through Jesus to bridge the gulf that separated me from you . . . forever. I was dead in my sins and mistakes. I will abide under the shadow of the cross where I have found safety. In Jesus' name, amen.

24

Jesus Asks John to Care for His Mother

When Jesus therefore saw His mother, and the disciple whom He loved
standing by, He said to His mother, "Woman, behold your son!"

John 19:26

M ary is older now. The hair at her temples is gray. Wrinkles have replaced her youthful skin. Her hands are calloused. She has raised a houseful of children. And now she beholds the crucifixion of her firstborn.

One wonders what memories she conjures up as she witnesses his torture. The long ride to Bethlehem, perhaps. A baby's bed made from cow's hay. Fugitives in Egypt. At home in Nazareth. Panic in Jerusalem. "I thought he was with you!" Carpentry lessons. Dinner table laughter.

And then the morning Jesus came in from the shop early, his eyes firmer, his voice more direct. He had heard the news. "John is preaching in the desert." Her son took off his nail apron, dusted off his hands, and with one last look said good-bye to his mother. They both knew it would never be the same again. In that last look they shared a secret, the full extent of which was too painful to say aloud.

Mary learned that day the heartache that comes from saying good-bye. From then on she was to love her son from a distance: on the edge of the crowd, outside of a packed house, on the shore of the sea. Maybe she was even there when the enigmatic promise was made, "Anyone who has left . . . mother . . . for my sake."

"Woman, behold your son!"

John fastened his arm around Mary a little tighter.

Jesus was asking him to be the son that a mother needs and that in some ways he never was.

Jesus looked at Mary. His ache was from a pain far greater than that of the nails and thorns. In their silent glance they again shared a secret. And he said good-bye.

No Wonder They Call Him the Savior

Lord Jesus, there are so many aspects to your life and death, such as your relationship with your mom, that leave me shaking my head and feeling it's a great mystery. Thank you for knowing the pain that we experience when we must say good-bye to someone we love so dearly. In your name, amen.

25

ABANDONED BY GOD

*Now from the sixth hour until the ninth hour
there was darkness over all the land.*

MATTHEW 27:45

Noises intermingle on the hill: Pharisees mocking, swords clanging, and dying men groaning. Jesus scarcely speaks. When he does, diamonds sparkle against velvet. He gives his killers grace and his mother a son. He answers the prayer of a thief.

Then, at midday, darkness falls like a curtain. This

is a supernatural darkness. Not a casual gathering of clouds or a brief eclipse of the sun. This is a three-hour blanket of blackness. Merchants in Jerusalem light candles. Soldiers ignite torches. The universe grieves. The sky weeps.

Christ lifts his heavy head and eyelids toward the heavens and spends his final energy crying out toward the ducking stars. "'Eli, Eli, lama sabachthani?' that is, 'My God, My God, why have You forsaken Me?'" (Matthew 27:46).

We would ask the same. Why him? Why forsake your Son? Forsake the murderers. Desert the evildoers. Turn your back on perverts and peddlers of pain. Abandon them, not him.

What did Christ feel on the cross? The icy displeasure of a sin-hating God. Why? Because he "carried our sins in his body" (1 Peter 2:24 NCV).

With hands nailed open, he invited God, "Treat me as you would treat them!" And God did. In an act that broke the heart of the Father, yet honored the holiness of heaven, sin-purging judgment flowed over the sinless Son of the ages.

And heaven gave earth her finest gift: the Lamb of God who took away the sin of the world.

"My God, My God, why have You forsaken Me?" Why did Christ scream those words? So you'll never have to.

3:16

Lamb of God, who takes away the sin of the world, thank you that I will never have to face the horror of feeling forsaken by the Father. My God, my God, thank you for receiving his sacrifice in my behalf. In Jesus' name, amen.

26

THIRSTY ON
THE CROSS

*Later, knowing that everything had now been finished, and so
that Scripture would be fulfilled, Jesus said, "I am thirsty."*

JOHN 19:28 NIV

This is the final act of Jesus' life. In the concluding
measure of his earthly composition, we hear the
sounds of a thirsty man.

And through his thirst—through a sponge and a jar
of cheap wine—he leaves a final appeal.

"You can trust me."

Jesus. Lips cracked and mouth of cotton. Throat so dry he couldn't swallow, and voice so hoarse he could scarcely speak. He is thirsty. Since tasting the cup of wine in the Upper Room twelve hours previous, Jesus has been beaten, spat upon, bruised, and cut. No liquid has salved his throat.

Why doesn't he do something about it? Couldn't he? Didn't he, with one word, banish the rain and calm the waves? Did God not say, "I will pour water on him who is thirsty" (Isaiah 44:3)?

If so, why does Jesus endure thirst?

While we are asking this question, add a few more. Why did he grow weary in Samaria (John 4:6), disturbed in Nazareth (Mark 6:6), and angry in the temple (John 2:15)? Why was he sleepy in the boat on the Sea of Galilee (Mark 4:38), sad at the tomb of Lazarus (John 11:35), and hungry in the wilderness (Matthew 4:2)?

And why, six hours earlier, had he refused a drink?

"They brought Jesus to the place called Golgotha

(which means The Place of the Skull). Then they offered him wine mixed with myrrh, but he did not take it" (Mark 15:22–23 NIV).

Before the nail was pounded, a drink was offered. Mark said the wine was mixed with myrrh. Matthew described it as wine mixed with gall. Both myrrh and gall contain sedative properties that numb the senses. But Jesus refused them. He refused to be stupefied by the drugs, opting instead to feel the full force of his suffering.

Why did he endure all these feelings? Because he knew you would feel them too.

He knew you would be weary, disturbed, and angry. He knew you'd be sleepy, grief-stricken, and hungry. He knew you'd face pain. If not the pain of the body, the pain of the soul . . . pain too sharp for any drug. He knew you'd face thirst. If not a thirst for water, at least a thirst for truth, and the truth we glean from the image of a thirsty Christ is—he understands.

And because he understands, we can come to him.

He Chose the Nails

Lord, thank you that because you have suffered so deeply, you understand—not just as God but as a human—everything that I have ever gone through and ever will go through. Thank you for opening up a new and living way for me to come freely before your throne to find help in every time of need. In Jesus' name, amen.

27

JESUS' LAST WORDS
ON THE CROSS

And about the ninth hour Jesus cried out with a loud
voice, saying, "Eli, Eli, lama sabachthani?" that is, "My
God, My God, why have You forsaken Me?"

MATTHEW 27:46

The hill is quiet now. Not still but quiet. For the first time all day there is no noise. The clamor began to subside when the darkness—that puzzling midday darkness—fell.

Like water douses a fire, the shadows doused the ridicule. No more taunts. No more jokes. No more jesting. And, in time, no more mockers. One by one the onlookers turned and began the descent.

We listened to the trio of dying men groaning. Hoarse, guttural, thirsty groans. They groaned with each rolling of the head and each pivot of the legs.

But as the minutes became hours, these groans diminished. The three seemed dead. Were it not for the belabored breathing, you would have thought they were.

Then he screamed. As if someone had yanked his hair, the back of his head slammed against the sign that bore his name, and he screamed. Like a dagger cuts the curtain, his scream cut the dark. Standing as straight as the nails would permit, he cried as one calling for a lost friend, "Eli!"

His voice was raspy, scratchy. Reflections of the torch flame danced in his wide eyes.

"My God!"

Ignoring the volcano of erupting pain, he pushed upward until his shoulders were higher than his nailed hands. "Why have you forsaken me?"

The soldiers stared. The weeping of the women ceased. One of the Pharisees sneered sarcastically, "He's calling Elijah."

No one laughed.

He'd shouted a question to the heavens, and you half expected heaven to shout one in return.

And apparently it did. For the face of Jesus softened, and an afternoon dawn broke as he spoke a final time. "It is finished. Father, into your hands I commit my spirit."

He Chose the Nails

Heavenly Father, I'm sure your heart broke when your Son cried out to you in such agony. My heart breaks as I read it. All because of sin. All because of me. Melt my heart to love you with all of my being. In Jesus' name, amen.

28

A CRY OF VICTORY

When he had received the drink, Jesus said, "It is finished."
With that, he bowed his head and gave up his spirit.

JOHN 19:30 NIV

It is finished."

Stop and listen. Can you imagine the cry from the cross? The sky is dark.

The other two victims are moaning. The jeering mouths are silent. Perhaps there is thunder. Perhaps there is weeping. Perhaps there is silence. Then Jesus draws in a deep breath, pushes his feet down on that Roman nail, and cries, "It is finished!"

What was finished?

The history-long plan of redeeming man was finished. The message of God to man was finished. The works done by Jesus as a man on earth were finished.

The task of selecting and training ambassadors was finished. The job was finished. The song had been sung. The blood had been poured. The sacrifice had been made. The sting of death had been removed. It was over.

A cry of defeat? Hardly. Had his hands not been fastened down, I dare say that a triumphant fist would have punched the dark sky. No, this is no cry of despair. It is a cry of completion. A cry of victory. A cry of fulfillment. Yes, even a cry of relief.

It's over.
An angel sighs. A star wipes away a tear.

"Take me home."
Yes, take him home.
Take this Prince to his King.
Take this Son to his Father.

Take this pilgrim to his home.
(He deserves a rest.)

"Take me home."
Come, ten thousand angels! Come and take this
    wounded troubadour to
the cradle of his Father's arms!
Farewell, manger's infant.
Bless you, holy ambassador.
Go home, death slayer.
Rest well, sweet soldier.

The battle is over.

No Wonder They Call Him the Savior

O Lord, conqueror over death, to hear you say "It is finished!" is glorious. I confess with my lips that there is nothing I can do or say that will add to what you did on the cross. You are my only hope of salvation. In Jesus' name, amen.

29

THE TEMPLE CURTAIN
IS TORN

But Jesus cried out again in a loud voice and died.
Then the curtain in the Temple was torn into
two pieces, from the top to the bottom.

MATTHEW 27:50—51 NCV

The curtain of the Temple was hung before the Holy of Holies, which was part of the Temple no one could enter. Jewish worshipers could enter the outer court, but only the priests could enter the Holy

Place. And no one, except the high priest on one day a year, entered the Holy of Holies. No one. Why? Because the shekinah glory—the glory of God—was present there.

No one but the high priest entered the Holy of Holies. *No one.* To do so meant death. In no uncertain terms, the curtain declared: "This far and no farther!"

What did fifteen hundred years of a curtain-draped Holy of Holies communicate? Simple. God is holy . . . separate from us and unapproachable. Even Moses was told, "You cannot see my face, because no one can see me and live" (Exodus 33:20 NCV). God is holy, and we are sinners, and there is a distance between us.

But Jesus hasn't left us with an unapproachable God. "There is one God and one mediator between God and men, the man Christ Jesus" (1 Timothy 2:5 NIV). When Jesus' flesh was torn on the cross, the curtain was torn in two.

It was as if the hands of heaven had been gripping the veil, waiting for this moment. One instant it was whole; the next it was ripped in two from top to bottom. No delay. No hesitation.

We are welcome to enter into God's presence—any

day, any time. God has removed the barrier that separates us from him. The barrier of sin? Down. No more curtain.

But we have a tendency to put the barrier back up with the curtain of our heart. Sometimes, no, oftentimes, we allow our mistakes and guilty conscience to keep us from God.

Don't allow a veil of guilt to keep you from your Father. Trust the cross. The curtain is down, the door is open, and you are welcome in God's presence.

He Chose the Nails

Loving Father, what a great day it was when the curtain was torn in two! Help me never to put that curtain back up in my heart. I draw near with confidence to your throne, knowing the way is paved by grace. In Jesus' name, amen.

30

THE CENTURION AT THE FOOT OF THE CROSS

When the centurion and those with him who were guarding
Jesus saw the earthquake and all that had happened, they were
terrified, and exclaimed, "Surely he was the Son of God!"

MATTHEW 27:54 NIV

The centurion was no stranger to finality. Over the years he'd grown callous to the screams of the crucified. He'd mastered the art of numbing his heart.

But this crucifixion plagued him. As the hours wore on, the centurion didn't know what to do with the Nazarene's silence. He didn't know what to do with his kindness. But most of all, he was perplexed by the darkness. He didn't know what to do with the black sky in midafternoon. No one could explain it . . . no one even tried. One minute the sun, the next the darkness.

When Jesus suddenly sliced the silence by calling out, "It is finished," it wasn't a scream. It was a roar . . . a lion's roar. From what world that roar came the centurion didn't know, but he knew it wasn't this one.

The centurion stood up and took a few paces toward the Nazarene. As he got closer, he could tell that Jesus was staring into the sky. There was something in his eyes that the soldier had to see. But after only a few steps, he fell. The ground was shaking, gently at first and now violently. He tried once more to walk and was able to take a few steps and then fall . . . at the foot of the cross.

He looked up into the face of this one near death. The King looked down at the crusty old centurion. Jesus' hands were fastened; they couldn't reach out. His feet were nailed to timber; they couldn't walk toward him. His head was heavy with pain; he could scarcely move it. But his eyes . . . they were afire.

They were unquenchable. They were the eyes of God.

Perhaps that is what made the centurion say what he said. He saw the eyes of God.

"It's all right," God's eyes said. "I've seen the storms and it's still all right."

The centurion's convictions began to flow together like rivers. "This was no carpenter," he spoke under his breath. "This was no peasant. This was no normal man."

He stood and looked around at the rocks that had fallen and the sky that had blackened. He turned and stared at the soldiers as they stared at Jesus with frozen faces. He turned and watched as the eyes of Jesus lifted and looked toward home. He listened as the parched lips parted and the swollen tongue spoke for the last time.

"Father, into your hands I commit my spirit."

Had the centurion not said it, the soldiers would

have. Had the centurion not said it, the rocks would have—as would have the angels, the stars, even the demons. But he did say it. It fell to a nameless foreigner to state what they all knew.

"Surely he was the Son of God."

Six Hours One Friday

Son of God, what a wonder you are! Even a hardened executioner could see the truth of who you were and confessed it with his lips. I will gladly join him today and confess that surely you are the Son of God. In your name, Jesus, amen.

31

AN ANCHOR FOR
YOUR SOUL

*This hope we have as an anchor of the soul, both sure and
steadfast, and which enters the Presence behind the veil.*

H E B R E W S   6 : 19

S ix hours, one Friday.

To the casual observer the six hours are
mundane. A shepherd with his sheep, a house-
wife with her thoughts, a doctor with his patients. But
to the handful of awestruck witnesses, the most mad-
dening of miracles is occurring.

God is on a cross. The Creator of the universe is being executed.

Spit and blood are caked to his cheeks, and his lips are cracked and swollen. Thorns rip his scalp. His lungs scream with pain. His legs knot with cramps. Taut nerves threaten to snap as pain twangs her morbid melody. Yet, death is not ready. And there is no one to save him, for he is sacrificing himself.

It is no normal six hours . . . it is no normal Friday.

For worse than the breaking of his body is the shredding of his heart.

His own countrymen clamor for his death.

His own disciple planted the kiss of betrayal.

His own friends ran for cover.

And now his own father is beginning to turn his back on him, leaving him alone.

Let me ask you a question: What do you do with that day in history? What do you do with its claims?

If it really happened . . . if God did commandeer his own crucifixion . . . if he did turn his back on his own Son . . . and if he did storm Satan's gate, then those six hours that Friday were packed with tragic triumph. If that was God on that cross, then the hill called Skull is granite studded with stakes to which you can anchor your soul forever.

Six Hours One Friday

Father, thank you that Jesus ascended into heaven and entered into your presence as the High Priest for all. Thank you that he not only administers the sacrifice but is the sacrifice himself. This is the anchor of my soul from which even the powers of darkness cannot budge me. In Jesus' name, amen.

32

FRIENDS TAKE
JESUS' BODY

Going to Pilate, [Joseph] asked for Jesus' body, and
Pilate ordered that it be given to him.

MATTHEW 27:58 NIV

They are coming as friends—secret friends—but friends nonetheless. "You can take him down now, soldier. I'll take care of him."

A soldier leans a ladder against the center tree, ascends it, and removes the stake that holds the beam to the upright part of the cross. Two of the other soldiers, glad that the day's work is nearing completion, assist with the heavy chore of laying the cypress crosspiece and body on the ground.

"Careful now," says Joseph.

The five-inch nails are wrenched from the hard wood. The body that encased a Savior is lifted and laid on a large rock.

"He's yours," says the sentry.

The two are not accustomed to this type of work. Yet their hands move quickly to their tasks.

Joseph of Arimathea kneels behind the head of Jesus and tenderly wipes the wounded face. With a soft, wet cloth he cleans the blood that came in the Garden, that came from the lashings and from the crown of thorns. With this done, he closes the eyes tight.

Nicodemus unrolls some linen sheeting that Joseph brought and places it on the rock beside the body. The two Jewish leaders lift the lifeless body of Jesus and set it on the linen. Parts of the body are now anointed with perfumed spices. As Nicodemus touches the cheeks of the Master with aloe, the emotion he has been containing escapes. His own tear falls on the face of the crucified King. He pauses to brush away another. The middle-aged Jew looks longingly at the young Galilean.

The high society of Jerusalem wasn't going to look too kindly on two of their religious leaders burying a revolutionist. But for Joseph and Nicodemus the choice was obvious. And, besides, they'd much rather save their souls than their skins.

3:16

Heavenly Father, who could touch your Son's lifeless body and not shed tears? I want to reach out and touch him as well and know just how much the story didn't end here. Thank you that Sunday was yet to come! In Jesus' name, amen.

33

JESUS' BURIAL

We know that when Jesus was raised from the dead it was a signal of the end of death-as-the-end. Never again will death have the last word. When Jesus died, he took sin down with him, but alive he brings God down to us.

ROMANS 6:9–10 MSG

When Pilate learned that Jesus was dead, he asked the soldiers if they were certain. They were. Had they seen the Nazarene twitch, had they heard even one moan, they would have broken his legs to speed his end. But there was no need. The thrust of a spear removed all doubt. The Romans knew their job. And their job was finished. They pried loose the nails, lowered his body, and gave it to Joseph and Nicodemus.

Joseph of Arimathea. Nicodemus the Pharisee. They sat in seats of power and bore positions of influence. Men of means and men of clout. But they would've traded it all for one breath out of the body of Jesus. He had answered the prayer of their hearts, the prayer for the Messiah. As much as the soldiers wanted him dead, even more these men wanted him alive.

As they sponged the blood from his beard, don't you know they listened for his breath? As they wrapped the cloth around his hands, don't you know they hoped for a pulse? Don't you know they searched for life?

But they didn't find it.

So they do with him what they were expected to do with a dead man. They wrap his body in clean linen and place it in a tomb. Joseph's tomb. Roman guards are stationed to guard the corpse. And a Roman seal is set on the rock of the tomb. For three days, no one gets close to the grave.

But then, Sunday arrives. And with Sunday comes

light—a light within the tomb. A bright light? A soft light? Flashing? Hovering? We don't know. But there was a light.

For he is the light. And with the light came life. Just as the darkness was banished, now the decay is reversed. Heaven blows and Jesus breathes. His chest expands. Waxy lips open. Wooden fingers lift. Heart valves swish and hinged joints bend.

And, as we envision the moment, we stand in awe.

We stand in awe not just because of what we see, but because of what we know.

When Christ Comes

O Lord, Author of my life, what was it like when your life reentered your body? May heaven blow and breathe that life into my spirit today. I stand in awe and worship you, almighty God. In Jesus' name, amen.

34

JOHN STAYED
CLOSE BY

They did not yet understand from the Scriptures
that Jesus must rise from the dead.

JOHN 20:9 NCV

Could there have been a greater tragedy for John than a dead Jesus? Three years earlier John had turned his back on his career and cast his lot with this Nazarene carpenter.

Earlier in the week John had enjoyed a ticker-tape parade as Jesus and the disciples entered Jerusalem. Oh, how quickly things had turned! The people who had called him king on Sunday called for his death the following Friday.

John didn't know on that Friday what you and I now know. He didn't know that Friday's tragedy would be Sunday's triumph. He didn't know.

That's why what he did on Saturday is so important. We don't know anything about this day; we have no passage to read, no knowledge to share.

All we know is this: When Sunday came, John was still present. When Mary Magdalene came looking for him, she found him.

Jesus was dead. The Master's body was lifeless. John's friend and future were buried. But John had not left. Why? Was he waiting for the resurrection? No. As far as he knew, the lips were forever silent and the hands forever still. He wasn't expecting a Sunday surprise. Then why was he here?

Perhaps the answer was pragmatic; perhaps he was taking care of Jesus' mother.

Or perhaps he didn't have anywhere else to go. Could be he didn't have any money or energy or direction . . . or all of the above.

Or maybe he lingered because he loved Jesus.

To others, Jesus was a miracle worker, a master teacher, the hope of Israel. But to John, he was all of these and more.

To John, Jesus was a friend.

You don't abandon a friend—not even when that friend is dead. John stayed close to Jesus.

He had a habit of doing this. He was close to Jesus in the Upper Room, in the Garden of Gethsemane, and at the foot of the cross. And he was a quick walk from the tomb at the burial.

Did he understand Jesus? No.

Was he glad Jesus did what he did? No.

But did he leave Jesus? No.

He Chose the Nails

My Lord and Savior, there's so much I don't understand, but I do understand that I can join John and spend the rest of my life loving you. Be to me all that you were to John . . . and more. In Jesus' name, amen.

35

THE EMPTY GRAVE

They were both running, but the other follower ran faster than Peter and reached the tomb first. He bent down and looked in and saw the strips of linen cloth lying there, but he did not go in.

JOHN 20:4–5 NCV

Very early on Sunday morning Peter and John were given the news: "Jesus' body is missing!" Instantly the two disciples hurried to the sepulcher, John outrunning Peter and arriving first. What he saw so stunned him he froze at the entrance.

What did he see? "Strips of linen cloth." The original Greek provides helpful insight here. John employs a term that means "rolled up," "still in their folds." These burial wraps had not been ripped off and thrown down. The linens were undisturbed. The grave clothes were still rolled and folded.

How could this be?

If friends or foes had removed the body, would they not have taken the clothes with it? If not, if for some reason friends or foes had unwrapped the body, would they have been so careful as to dispose of the clothing in such an orderly fashion? Of course not!

But if neither friend nor foe took the body, who did?

This was John's question, and this question led to John's discovery. "He saw and believed" (John 20:8 NCV).

Through the rags of death, John saw the power of life. Odd, don't you think, that God would use something as sad as a burial wrap to change a life?

But God is given to such practices:

In his hand, empty wine jugs at a wedding become a symbol of power.

A crude manger in Bethlehem is his symbol of devotion.

And a tool of death is a symbol of his love.

3:16

Gracious God, I would love to have seen the look on John's face at the moment when the light went on and he believed that Jesus was alive. Refresh my faith with the same sense of wonder and surprise. You are alive. I believe! In Jesus' name, amen.

36

MARY MAGDALENE
AT JESUS' TOMB

But Mary stood outside by the tomb weeping . . .

JOHN 20:11

A party was the last thing Mary Magdalene expected as she approached the tomb on that Sunday morning. The last few days had brought nothing to celebrate. To her the last few days had brought nothing but tragedy.

In the early morning mist she arises from her mat, takes her spices and aloes, and leaves her house, past the Gate of Gennath and up to the hillside. She anticipates a somber task. By now the body will be swollen. Death's odor will be pungent.

A gray sky gives way to gold as she walks up the narrow trail. As she rounds the final bend, she gasps. The rock in front of the grave is pushed back.

When she stoops down and sticks her head into the hewn entrance, she sees what looks to be a man, but he's white—radiantly white. He is one of two lights on either end of the vacant slab.

"Why are you crying?" An uncommon question to be asked in a cemetery. In fact, the question is rude. That is, unless the questioner knows something the questionee doesn't.

"They have taken my Lord away, and I don't know where they have put him."

She still calls him "my Lord." As far as she knows his lips were silent. As far as she knows, his corpse had been carted off by grave robbers. But in spite of it all, he is still her Lord.

Such devotion moves Jesus. It moves him closer to her. So close she hears him breathing. She turns and there he stands. She thinks he is the gardener.

"Why are you crying? Who is it you are looking for?" (John 20:15 NIV).

He doesn't leave her wondering long, just long enough to remind us that he loves to surprise us. He waits for us to despair of human strength and then intervenes with heavenly. God waits for us to give up and then—surprise!

And listen to the surprise as Mary's name is spoken by a man she loved—a man she had buried.

"Miriam."

God appearing at the strangest of places. Doing the strangest of things. Stretching smiles where there had hung only frowns. Placing twinkles where there were only tears. Hanging a bright star in a dark sky. Arching rainbows in the midst of thunderclouds. Calling names in a cemetery.

"Miriam," he said softly, "surprise!"

Mary was shocked. It's not often you hear your name spoken by an eternal tongue. But when she did, she recognized it. And when she did, she responded correctly. She worshiped him.

Six Hours One Friday

Dear Lord, I ask you to help me hear your voice and see you in the unexpected moments of life. You are my Lord just as much as you were Mary's. I am looking for you today and can hardly wait to be surprised. In Jesus' name, amen.

37

THE DISCIPLES
GATHER

They . . . found the eleven and those who were with them gathered
together, saying, "The Lord is risen indeed, and has appeared to Simon!"

LUKE 24:33—34

No one knows what happened to the disciples in the hours after they ran away when Jesus was arrested. Those hours are left to speculation. Any guilt, any fear, any doubts are all unrecorded.

But we do know one thing. They came back. Slowly. One by one. Matthew, Nathaniel, Andrew. They came out of hiding. James, Peter, Thaddeus. From all sections of the city they appeared.

Too convicted to go home, yet too confused to go on. Each with a desperate hope that it had all been a nightmare or a cruel joke. Each hoping to find some kind of solace in numbers. They came back. Something in their nature refused to let them give up. Something in those words spoken by the Master pulled them back together.

I guess we've all been there. I dare say that all of us have witnessed our sandcastle promises swept away by the pounding waves of panic and insecurity. I imagine that all of us have seen our words of promise and obedience ripped into ribbons by the chainsaw of fear and fright. We've all walked the street of Jerusalem in the shadows.

What made them return? Rumors of the resurrection? That had to be a part of it. Those who walked next to Jesus had learned to expect him to do the unusual. You just don't pack up the bags and go home after three years of seeing all they had seen.

Maybe he really had risen from the dead.

But it was more than just rumors of an empty tomb. They had betrayed their Master, and now they were having to deal with the shame. Seeking forgiveness, but not knowing where to look for it, they came back. Each with a scrapbook full of memories and a thin thread of hope.

And just when the gloom gets good and thick, a familiar face walks through the wall. My, what an ending. Or, better said, what a beginning! Come out of the shadows! Be done with your hiding! A repentant heart is enough to summon the Son of God himself to walk through our walls of guilt and shame. He who forgave his followers stands ready to forgive the rest of us. All we have to do is come back.

No Wonder They Call Him the Savior

Father, thank you that you have no problem walking through the walls that I sometimes hide behind. I welcome you to come with your forgiveness and shed your light and joy into my life. In Jesus' name, amen.

38

"Peace Be with You"

Then, the same day at evening, being the first day of the week, when the doors were shut where the disciples were assembled, for fear of the Jews, Jesus came and stood in the midst, and said to them, "Peace be with you."

JOHN 20:19

The church of Jesus Christ began with a group of frightened men in a second-floor room in Jerusalem. Though they'd marched with him for three years, their most courageous act now was to get up and lock the door.

It was an hour for self-examination. All their efforts

seemed so futile. When the Roman soldiers took Jesus, Jesus' followers took off. With the very wine of the covenant on their breath and the bread of his sacrifice in their bellies, they fell.

All the boasts of bravado and declarations of devotion lay broken and shattered at the gate of Gethsemane's garden.

We don't know where the disciples went when they fled the Garden, but we do know they took the heart-stopping memory of a man who called himself no less than God in the flesh. And they couldn't get him out of their minds. As a result, they came back, and the church of our Lord began with a group of frightened men in an upper room.

Sound familiar? How many churches have just enough religion to come together, but not enough passion to go out? Good people. Plenty of good intentions. Budgets. Meetings. Words. Promises. But while all this is going on, the door remains locked and the story stays a secret.

Upper-room futility. Confused ambassadors behind locked doors. What will it take to unlock them? What will it take to ignite the fire? What will it take to restore the first-century passion?

What is needed to get us out is exactly what unlocked the doors of the apostles' hearts: they saw Jesus, who said to them and to us, "Peace be with you." The stone of the tomb could not keep him in. The walls of the room could not keep him out.

Their sins collided with their Savior, and their Savior won!

Allow Jesus to come into your upper room and stand before you. Run your fingers over his feet. Place your hand in the pierced side. And look into those eyes. Those same eyes that melted the gates of hell and sent Satan running. Look at them as they look at you. You'll never be the same.

Six Hours One Friday

My Lord and Savior, here I am. Just me. Help me to see you, really see you, even your eyes, and to hear your voice speaking words of peace. Ignite a fresh fire in my heart. In Jesus' name, amen.

39

HIS RESURRECTED
BODY

*He said to Thomas, "Reach your finger here, and look
at My hands; and reach your hand here, and put it into
My side. Do not be unbelieving, but believing."*

JOHN 20:27

Jesus appeared to the followers in a flesh-and-bone
body: "A spirit does not have flesh and bones as you
see that I have" (Luke 24:39 NASB). His resurrected
body was a real body, real enough to walk on the road

to Emmaus, to be mistaken for that of a gardener, to swallow fish at breakfast.

In the same breath, Jesus' real body was really different.

The Emmaus disciples didn't recognize him, and walls didn't stop him. Mark tried to describe the new look and settled for "[Jesus] appeared in another form" (Mark 16:12). While his body was the same, it was better; it was glorified. It was a heavenly body.

And I can't find the passage that says he shed it. He ascended in it.

"He was lifted up while they were looking on, and a cloud received Him out of their sight" (Acts 1:9 NASB). He will return in it. The angel told the followers, "This Jesus, who has been taken up from you into heaven, will come in just the same way as you have watched Him go into heaven" (Acts 1:11 NASB).

The God-man is still both. The hands that blessed the bread of the boy now bless the prayers of the millions. And the mouth that commissions angels is the mouth that kissed children.

You know what this means? The greatest force in

the cosmos understands and intercedes for you. "We have an Advocate with the Father, Jesus Christ the righteous" (I John 2:1 NASB).

Next Door Savior

Jesus Christ, the Righteous One, thank you for being my Advocate before the Father's throne. I am delighted to be in your hands, under the shelter of your wings. Bless and praise you for your intercession over my life. In your name, amen.

40

HE DID IT JUST
FOR YOU

Jesus said to him, "Thomas, because you have seen Me, you have believed. Blessed are those who have not seen and yet have believed."

JOHN 20:29

When God entered time and became a man, he who was boundless became bound. Imprisoned in flesh. Restricted by weary-prone muscles and eyelids. For more than three decades, his once-limitless reach would be limited to the stretch of an arm, his speed checked to the pace of human feet.

Was he ever tempted to reclaim his boundlessness? In the middle of a long trip, did he ever consider transporting himself to the next city? When the heat parched his lips, did he give thought to popping over to the Caribbean for some refreshment?

If ever he entertained such thoughts, he never gave in to them. Not once did Christ use his supernatural powers for personal comfort. With a wave of his hand, he could've boomeranged the spit of his accusers back into their faces. With an arch of his brow, he could've paralyzed the hand of the soldier as he braided the crown of thorns. But he didn't.

Want to know the coolest thing about the coming?

Not that the One who played marbles with the stars gave it up to play marbles with marbles. Or that the One who hung the galaxies gave it up to hang doorjambs to the displeasure of a cranky client who wanted everything yesterday but couldn't pay for anything until tomorrow.

Not that he, in an instant, went from needing

nothing to needing air, food, a tub of hot water and salts for his tired feet, and, more than anything, needing somebody—anybody—who was more concerned about where he would spend eternity than where he would spend Friday's paycheck.

Or that he resisted the urge to fry the two-bit, self-appointed hall monitors of holiness who dared suggest that he was doing the work of the devil.

Not that he kept his cool while the dozen best friends he ever had felt the heat and got out of the kitchen. Or that he gave no command to the angels who begged, "Just give the nod, Lord. One word and these demons will be deviled eggs."

Not that he refused to defend himself when blamed for every sin of every slut and sailor since Adam. Or that he stood silent as a million guilty verdicts echoed in the tribunal of heaven and the giver of light was left in the chill of a sinner's night.

Not even that after three days in a dark hole he stepped into the Easter sunrise with a smile and a swagger and a question for lowly Lucifer—"Is that your best punch?"

That was cool, incredibly cool.

But the coolest thing about the One who gave up the crown of heaven for a crown of thorns: He did it for you. Just for you.

He Chose the Nails

Heavenly Father, I'm glad that I don't have to understand all that Jesus did in order to believe because I really don't understand this magnificent love. But I am so glad to believe in him, so glad he wore the crown of thorns for me. I want to live for you alone today. In Jesus' name, amen.

SOURCES INDEX

All of the material for *On Calvary's Hill* was originally published in books authored by Max Lucado. All copyrights to the original works are held by Max Lucado.

And the Angels Were Silent (Nashville: Thomas Nelson, 1992): introduction, chapters 1, 2, 3, 7, 10.

A Gentle Thunder (Nashville: Thomas Nelson, 1995): chapter 8.

He Still Moves Stones (Nashville: Thomas Nelson, 1993, 1999): chapter 9.

When Christ Comes (Nashville: Thomas Nelson, 1999): chapter 33.

He Chose the Nails (Nashville: Thomas Nelson, 2000): chapters 13, 14, 17, 23, 26, 27, 29, 34, 40.

Just Like Jesus (Nashville: Thomas Nelson, 1998, 2003): chapter 4.

Next Door Savior (Nashville: Thomas Nelson, 2003): chapters 12, 39.

No Wonder They Call Him the Savior (Nashville: Thomas Nelson, 1986, 2004): chapters 5, 11, 19, 21, 22, 24, 28, 37.

Six Hours One Friday (Nashville: Thomas Nelson, 1989, 2004): chapters 20, 30, 31, 36, 38.

3:16 (Nashville: Thomas Nelson, 2007): chapters 6, 16, 18, 25, 32, 35.

Great Day Every Day (Nashville: Thomas Nelson, 2007, 2012): chapter 15.